THE RABBIT AND BEAR BOOKS:

1. Rabbit's Bad Habits
2. The Pest in the Nest
3. Attack of the Snack
4. A Bite in the Night
5. A Bad King is a Sad Thing

coming soon:

6. This Lake is Fake!

CW01620072

RABBIT & BEAR

The Pest in the Nest

STORY BY
JULIAN GOUGH

ILLUSTRATIONS BY
JIM FIELD

Hodder Children's Books

HODDER CHILDREN'S BOOKS

First published in Great Britain in 2017
by Hodder and Stoughton

10

A CIP catalogue record for this book
is available from the British Library.

ISBN: **9781292452982**

Printed in the UK by Bell & Bain Ltd, Glasgow.

This edition printed under license from Hodder and Stoughton

Hodder Children's Books
An imprint of
Hachette Children's Group
Part of Hodder and Stoughton
Carmelite House
50 Victoria Embankment
London EC4Y 0DZ

An Hachette UK Company
www.hachette.co.uk

www.hachettechildrens.co.uk

Dedicated to Farnborough Library.
From picture books at 2 years old,
to discovering new music at 22 years old.

Thank you for being there.

J.F.

●

For my mother, Elizabeth Gough (who is called Betty, and was a Grogan until she married my dad).

I was not the world's easiest child to put to bed, but she read me my bedtime stories with great patience, even when I wanted *The Saggy Baggy Elephant* for the fifty-seventh time.

Thanks, Mum.

J.G.

THREE SISTER MOUNTAINS
THE CLIFF OF A THOUSAND BIRDS
BEAR'S CAVE
WOODPECKER'S TREE
RABBIT'S WARREN
GIANT SANDPIT
THE FLOWER CLEARING

THUNDER MOUNTAINS
THIS WAY TO MONSTERS (DRAGONS! SKOOKUMS! HUMANS!)
N
W
E
S
WILD FOOL FALLS
WOLF WOODS
BIG PINE ISLAND
SMALL ISLAND
THE LONG LAKE
PEBBLE BEACH
TINY MOSS ISLAND (A ROCK)
THE BOG OF FROGS
THIS WAY TO OCEAN

Rabbit was having a lovely sleep in his friend Bear's cave, when a TERRIBLE noise woke him.

Oh no! thought Rabbit. Thunder! He opened his eyes. The cave was full of light.

Oh no! thought Rabbit. Lightning!

But the light was just sunshine, coming into the cave. And the noise was just Bear, snoring VERY LOUDLY.

Rabbit tried to cover his ears with his paws, but his ears were very big, and his paws were rather small.

"Oh, this is IMPOSSIBLE," said Rabbit, and hopped out of Bear's cave.

Outside, the winter snow was gone, except for two teeny, tiny piles of old, tired snow. On each pile rested two pinecones, a curved stick, and a carrot.

Our snowmen have melted, thought Rabbit.

And then he had a thought
so big that it filled him up, so
he had to stand on his tiptoes
and push out his chest.
Spring has sprung!
thought Rabbit.

At last!

Time to go home to his burrow. He had enjoyed a cosy winter with his friend Bear, but that snoring was driving him nuts.

Rabbit hopped down Bear's big hill, and up Rabbit's little hill.

Hmmm. His burrow looked a bit scruffy after the winter.

Better do some spring cleaning, thought Rabbit, and hopped into his burrow.

Oh, his burrow was REALLY scruffy. Lots of twigs, old leaves … Rabbit scooped out the mess with his paws, to reveal …

Hmmm. Was it a big rock? The root of a tree? … Wait a minute, it had eyes!

"AaaAAAAaaah!" shouted Rabbit so loudly that he hurt his own ears.

The two little eyes popped open and looked straight into Rabbit's eyes.

"Hulllllooooo Rrrrraaabbiittt," said the animal, incredibly slowly, with a long sigh.

Whew! It wasn't a snake.
"Oh, it's you, Tortoise,"
said Rabbit. "Get out,
I want to be alone."

"Is it ...

nnnneeeext year ...

alllllllreadyyyyy?"

asked Tortoise.

"Yes!" said Rabbit. "And it's already far too noisy! PEACE AND QUIET," he shouted, "THAT'S ALL I WANT." Owch. He had hurt his own ears again.

CARROT
D.C.M HOWE SEED C

"Aaaaallll right Rrrrrabbbbittt," said Tortoise, and walked out of the burrow so slowly that Rabbit thought he would go mad.

Tortoise finally got all the way outside, and fell asleep at once in the sunshine.

"Whew," said Rabbit, and sat on the sleeping Tortoise.

Rabbit stretched in the sunshine. Ah, peace! Ah, quiet!

BANG! BANG! BANG!

Rabbit jumped so high he scared himself.

(Rabbit was afraid of heights.)

"Oh my nerves!" he said when he had landed again. He looked all around. Nothing.

BANG! BANG! BANG!
BANG! BANG! BANG!

Rabbit looked down.

Nothing …

Rabbit looked up.

Something!!!

What. On earth.

Was that?

"Bear!" shouted Rabbit. "Bear, come here! Something Simply Has To Be Done!"

Bear wandered down the hill from her cave, rubbing her eyes with a big paw.

"Look!" said Rabbit, and pointed straight up.

Bear looked. "Sorry," she said. "I can't see very well. It looks like a blur."

"It IS a blur," said Rabbit.

All the way up near the top of the tree, a green blur went ...

BANG! BANG!
BANG! BANG!

Big bits of bark fell down, and landed on Bear and Rabbit.

"My fur!" said Rabbit, shaking off the bits of bark.

"This is completely impossible."

Far above them, the blur stopped banging. Suddenly it wasn't blurry any more.

"It's a bird," said Bear.

"It's a pest," said Rabbit.

"Hey! Hey hey hey! I'm a Woodwoodwoodpecker," Woodpecker shouted down at them. "I'm not a pest. I EAT pests." She licked wriggly beetle grubs out of a hole in the tree with a long sticky, spiky tongue. "WOW WOW WOW," said the ex-blur, "these are DELICIOUS! Ha ha ha ha ha!"

"Why," shouted Rabbit, "are you laughing?"

"Because I'm happy! Happy happy happy!" said Woodpecker, and began to peck at the wood again.

"How lovely," said Bear. "We've never had a woodpecker in the valley."

"LOVELY?! She's so noisy, and happy, it's driving me crazy," said Rabbit.

Indeed, the new arrival was so noisy that Tortoise woke. He stood up. Rabbit fell off.

"Hey!" said Rabbit.

"Hulllllooooo again Rrrrraaabbiittt," said Tortoise. "Is it … nnnneeeext year … aaagaaain … alllllllreadyyyyy?"

"No!" said Rabbit. "It's only five minutes later!"

"Oooohhh …" said Tortoise with a sigh. "How saaaadddd … I'm a hundred years ooooooollld, you know. Or possibly … a hundred … and one …" And Tortoise fell asleep.

"Gah! He's driving me crazy too," said Rabbit.

"But Tortoise is sad, and quiet," said Bear.

"Yes! And it's driving me crazy!"

Bear thought about this. "So noisy, happy things drive you crazy?"

"Yes!"

"And quiet, sad things
drive you crazy?"

"Yes! Yes!" said Rabbit.

Bear thought about this some more. "But ... the only thing those things have in common," she said, scratching her head, "... is you."

Rabbit gave Bear a Look. "So?"

"Well," said Bear, "I think the creature that is driving you crazy isn't Woodpecker. And it isn't Tortoise. It's ..."

Hmmm. Bear didn't want to say it. Rabbit had a FIERCE temper.

"It's YOU, isn't it Bear?" said Rabbit, and raised his right foot to kick Bear.

"Er, no," said Bear. "It's you."

"I'M driving MYSELF crazy?" said Rabbit, shocked. He raised his left foot, to kick himself. But he had forgotten to put his right foot back down first, so he fell over.

"Yes," said Bear, "You see? Your Brain is getting into a fight with the World."

"I'm not getting into a fight with the World!" said Rabbit, standing up. "NOT!" Rabbit raised his foot, again, to kick Bear.

Hmmm, thought Rabbit, Bear is very Big. Maybe not.

So Rabbit kicked Tortoise instead. It was like kicking a big, sleepy rock, and it hurt his foot, a lot. "Owwa!" said Rabbit.

"Hmmm mmmmm?" said Tortoise quietly, and fell back to sleep.

Woodpecker pecked.

BANG! BANG! BANG!

"Aaargh!" said Rabbit. "EVERYTHING'S driving me crazy! But especially HER!"

And Rabbit picked up a pinecone and threw it straight up at Woodpecker.

Now, rabbits
are not great at
throwing things;
and the pinecone
missed Woodpecker,

and fell straight
back down, and hit
Rabbit in the eye.

"Owwa!" said Rabbit. "Look what she just did!"

Bear thought she had better do something, before Rabbit exploded.

"Er, Woodpecker," Bear shouted up the tree. "If you could peck more quietly ..."

"Then it would take longer. Much longer. Much much longer," shouted Woodpecker, who found it very hard to stop once she had got going. "MUCH MUCH MUCH …"

"Er, yes," shouted Bear. "I understand. OK, so if you could peck faster, then, perhaps, and get it over with ..."

"STOP SHOUTING!" shouted Rabbit.

"Can't peck any faster than this!" shouted Woodpecker, pecking to demonstrate.

… her head became a green blur again.

"Er, yes," shouted Bear, "I understand."

Woodpecker stopped pecking and looked around. "Wow! What a view!" she shouted. "I'm going to love love love it here!"

"There MUST be one somewhere," said Rabbit, looking around.

"What are you looking for?" said Bear.

"A rock. A big one. To throw at that Woodpecker menace."

"Why don't we help her, instead?" said Bear.

"HELP her?"

"Yes, help her."

"Help her DRIVE ME CRAZY?" said Rabbit. "What kind of friend are YOU?"

"No," said Bear. "Help her finish her job faster, so she doesn't drive you crazy."

"No way!" said Rabbit.

"Well then," said Bear, "I will." And Bear began to climb the tree.

"Traitor!" said Rabbit.

Bear stopped climbing and scratched her head.

"What's a traitor?" she asked.

"A Traitor," said Rabbit, glaring up at Bear, "is someone who Leaves a Friend to Help an Enemy!"

Bear sighed. "I really don't think Woodpecker is an enemy, Rabbit. Just let me go up and see."

Bear was rather good at climbing trees, because she practised a lot, looking for honey.

The world quickly got bigger, and brighter, and lighter, and airier, the higher Bear climbed. And Bear's problems seemed to get smaller, and less important, and further away …

"Hullo Woodpecker," said Bear quietly, when she had got to the top. "Are you an Enemy?"

"No! No no no no no no no," said Woodpecker, shaking her head. "I'm just trying to make a hole, in this tree, for my nest."

"Ah!" said Bear. "Well, that's going to take you a while, one little peck at a time. Let me help you."

"Sure!" said Woodpecker, and moved politely along the branch.

Bear stretched out her claws until they were as long as possible, and scraped away at the hole with all her strength. But the wood was very hard, and she could hardly scratch it.

"Oh dear," said Bear. "I'm afraid you're better at this than I am."

"Practice! Practice! Practice!" said Woodpecker. "You get very good at something if you do it all the time."

"True," said Bear, and looked around. What a view!

Woodpecker went back to work with her incredibly hard beak, as sharp as a chisel.

Bear sighed, and began to climb back down.

"Please, stay a while," said Woodpecker politely.

"Well, I don't want to be in your way," said Bear. "And also, er, it's very loud, right beside you."

"Oh, I'm taking a break," said Woodpecker. "To stretch my neck. It gets stiff."

"Oh, good," said Bear. "Rabbit!" she shouted down. "You should come up here. You'd love it. It would be very good for you."

"You're crazy too!" shouted Rabbit. "Rabbits don't climb trees! If you think I'm going to climb that tree you're more nuts than a million acorns!"

"Are you happy down there?" shouted Bear.

Rabbit wanted to shout Yes! just to annoy Bear. But deep down Rabbit was an honest rabbit. "No," he said, very quietly.

Bear climbed all the way back down the tree.

"Pardon?" said Bear.

"No," said Rabbit, more loudly. "I'm not happy."

"Then let me give you a lift," said Bear. "Hang on tight."

Rabbit grabbed Bear's thick fur and hung on tight, while Bear climbed back up the tall, tall tree.

"Are you scared?" said Bear, when they'd reached the top.

"No," said Rabbit. "Er … Have we left the ground yet?"

Bear looked over her shoulder; Rabbit's eyes were tightly shut.

Bear chuckled.

"Look," she said.

And Rabbit opened his eyes. "Wow," he said.

"That's what I always say!" said Woodpecker. "Wow wow wow wow wow wow …"

"Hey!" said Rabbit. "Mountains! Wait … There are mountains behind the mountains! And …" His rabbit eyes were having trouble even focusing that far away.

"… There are mountains behind the mountains behind the mountains!"

The tree swayed in the wind, and Rabbit swayed with it. Rabbit felt like he was part of the tree; and the tree was part of the forest; and the forest was part of the world.

"It's nice nice nice, isn't it," said Woodpecker.

"Wow," said Rabbit very quietly. "I thought the world was Small, and full of Me; but it is Big and not full of me at all."

"Yes," said Bear.

"Yes yes yes," said Woodpecker.

"Maybe my problems are not so big after all," said Rabbit.

"I think you are right," said Bear.

They climbed back down.

"I don't understand," said Rabbit. "I feel calm. And happy."

"Me too," said Bear. "But then, I usually do."

Rabbit looked up at the tree. "I can't believe I have learned Wisdom from a bird with a brain the size of a walnut," he said. "A brain that it bangs off a tree all day."

"I don't think you found the Wisdom in Woodpecker," said Bear.

"Ah! I found it in you, Bear!" said Rabbit, and hugged Bear.

"No," said Bear. "You found it ... in you."

"This is great!" said Rabbit. "Now I'll be Calm and Happy and Wise forever!" He lay down in the sunshine, totally relaxed, and put up his feet on Tortoise, who was still asleep.

"Maybe not forever," said Bear, who knew Rabbit rather well. "Unless you Practise."

"Nonsense!" said Rabbit. "I've changed forever!"

At the top of the tree, Woodpecker finished her break, and fluffed up her feathers, and started digging the hole for her nest again.

BANG! BANG! BANG!
BANG! BANG! BANG!

Rabbit jumped
twice his own height.
"AaaaaAAAAaargh!"

"What?" asked Bear.

"I'm angry! And I want to be calm! So I'm angry that I'm angry!" And Rabbit kicked himself, and fell over.

"Why did you kick yourself?"

"Because I'm annoyed with myself!" said Rabbit. "Because I can't change myself!"

"But you can change your thoughts," said Bear.

"Change my thoughts? What's wrong with them? My thoughts are PERFECT," said Rabbit.

"But your thoughts are making you unhappy," said Bear.

"No!" said Rabbit. "The world is making me unhappy! I must change the world!"

A little cloud passed in front of the sun. Rabbit threw a stone at it. "Stupid world! Change!"

But the world didn't change.

"Maybe you could just think about the world differently," said Bear. "Maybe you could … accept it."

"Accept! Accept!" said Rabbit. "… What's accept mean?"

"Saying, well, that's just the way it is," said Bear. "Not try to change it."

"No!" said Rabbit.

Rabbit seemed so certain. Maybe Bear was wrong. Maybe Rabbit was just too different from Bear, and Bear was being silly. Bear looked down at her feet, a bit embarrassed. Then she noticed her feet were doing something odd. So were Rabbit's.

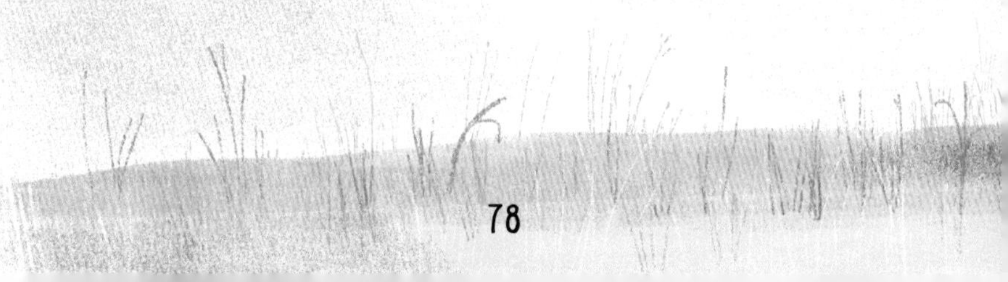

Bear's feet, and
Rabbit's feet,
were tapping the
ground, in rhythm
with Woodpecker's
pecking.

"Look, your feet have already accepted it," said Bear.

"Traitors!" Rabbit shouted at his feet.

But his feet kept tapping.

"I think your Body and your Mind are divided," said Bear, whose body and mind were not very often divided.

"Of course they are!" said Rabbit. "My mind is up here, being clever, and my body is down there, being stupid! I don't want my lovely mind to have anything to do with my stupid body!"

"Now, I think that is where you might be going wrong," said Bear.

"Wrong! WRONG! Me, WRONG?!" shouted Rabbit.

"What did you learn up the tree?" said Bear.

"Oh yes," said Rabbit. He remembered swaying in the branches of the treetop, a very small Rabbit in a very

big World. "Wow!" he said, remembering. And he stopped fighting the World. And he stopped fighting himself. And in that moment, he accepted everything.

WOW
WOW
WOW
WOW
WOW

said Rabbit.

BANG!
BANG!
BANG!
BANG!
BANG!

said Woodpecker.

THUMP
THUMP
THUMP
THUMP
THUMP

said Rabbit's feet.

ZZZZZZZZZ
ZZZZZZZZzz

said Tortoise.

And together, they all made music, and it was beautiful.

And Bear was so happy to see her friend look so happy that she began to sing. She made up the words as she went along.

"Spring!" she sang. "Spring! Is a Wonderful, Funderful Thing!"

There was a tiny growl of thunder, from the little cloud. Next time around, she sang, "Spring! Spring! Is a Wonderful, Thunderful Thing!"

Soon it would rain, and the plants would begin to grow, and Spring would have Sprung. But right now they were dancing and their minds and their bodies were one.

And first Mole ... then Mouse ... then Vole ... and, one by one, all the animals of the forest came out to dance to the amazing music.

The sun came out from behind the cloud, and Bear sang, "Spring! Is a wonderful, Sunderful thing!"

BANG!BANG! WOW!WOW! THUMP!THUMP! ZZZZzzzz …

Bear shared the food she had stored in her cave. She even fed Wolf, so that Wolf wouldn't get hungry and eat the other dancers.

And they danced and feasted all day long, until it was dark, and Woodpecker was finished pecking a hole in the hard wood of the tree.

"Wow," said Rabbit, yawning. "That was the best party ever."

"Yes," said Bear, yawning.

"I don't want it to be over!" said Rabbit. "I hate silence! I want Woodpecker to keep going all night! All tomorrow! All week! Forever!"

"Well," said Bear sleepily, "now that the hole is finished, the nest will soon be full of little woodpeckers. And they will grow up fast, and need somewhere to live. More wood pecking. More parties."

"You're right,"
said Rabbit sleepily.
"Goodnight, Bear."

"Oh dear," said Tortoise, "is it thaaaaat time alreadyyyyy? It will take me aaaaages to get home ..."

"That's OK," said Rabbit. "You can sleep in my burrow, with me."

And soon Bear was asleep in her cave, and Woodpecker was asleep in her nest,

and Tortoise was asleep next to Rabbit, in Rabbit's burrow.

SNNNOOORRRE

said Bear loudly in her cave.

Down in his burrow, Rabbit heard Bear snoring, and started to get angry out of habit.

But the snoring wasn't really very loud.

Hmm, maybe I should think about it in a Different Way, thought Rabbit. Yes! I shall stop thinking of it as a Nasty Noise. I shall think of it instead as a nice, friendly reminder that my friend Bear is nearby.

And suddenly the sound, without changing at all, made Rabbit feel all happy and warm.

Yes, spring … is a wonderful … thing, thought Rabbit. And tomorrow is … is … going to be … a beautiful day … with my old friend Bear … and my new friend Woodpecker … Yes, tomorrow is … izzz … izzzzzzzzz … And Rabbit fell into his deepest, calmest sleep ever.

ZZZZZZZZZZZZ

ZZZZZZZZzzz

JULIAN GOUGH

© Andreas Riemenschneider 2015

Julian Gough is an award-winning novelist, playwright, poet, musician and scriptwriter.
He was born in London, grew up in Ireland and now lives in Berlin.

Among many other things, Julian wrote the ending to **Minecraft**, the world's most successful computer game for children of all ages.

Jim Field is an award-winning illustrator, character designer and animation director.
He grew up in Farnborough, worked in London and now lives in Paris.

His first picture book, **Cats Ahoy!**, written by Peter Bently, won the Booktrust Roald Dahl Funny Prize. He is perhaps best known for drawing frogs on logs in the bestselling **Oi Frog**.

He likes playing the guitar and drinking coffee.

JIM FIELD

© Sandy Foucherand 2016

LOOK OUT FOR MORE

RABBIT & BEAR

BOOKS COMING SOON!

FIND OUT WHAT HAPPENS NEXT IN:

ATTACK OF THE SNACK

'*Rabbit's Bad Habits* is a breath of fresh air in children's fiction, a laugh-out-loud story of rabbit and wolf and bear, of avalanches and snowmen. The sort of story that makes you want to send your children to bed early, so you can read it to them.'

Neil Gaiman

'A perfect animal double-act enchants.'

Alex O'Connell, *The Times* book of the week

'Sure to become a firm favourite.'

The Bookbag

'What a treat this little book is! Not only does it have a funny and warm story that is full of heart, it is also gorgeously presented … Lots of fun, highly recommended.'

Reading Zone